Hope

Flute and Piano Duet

Xavier Hersom

For public performance permission, contact Xavier Hersom at
xavierhersommusic@gmail.com

CONTENTS

Program Note

"Hope" was composed in 2020 during the height of the COVID-19 pandemic. It is a simple, yet beautiful duet for flute and piano. The evolving melody passing between the instruments represents life's changing tides. There are periods that are graceful and pensive and others that are fleeting and exciting. The end of the piece is grave like looming depression, but it finally resolves in a bright cord—this symbolizes how even as we face difficult situations in life, there is always hope.

Performance Note

This piece is idiomatic and can be enjoyed by many performers. The flute and piano are equally important and complement each other. The slurs give the effect of gentle, overlapping waves and the flute in measures 48-53 represents a rushing stream. The piano finishes the piece as if the weight of the world is on one's shoulders, but it finally ends in an unexpected hopeful chord like the sun breaking through the clouds.

Duration: ca. 2' 10"

Grade 3

Score

Score

Hope

Xavier Hersom

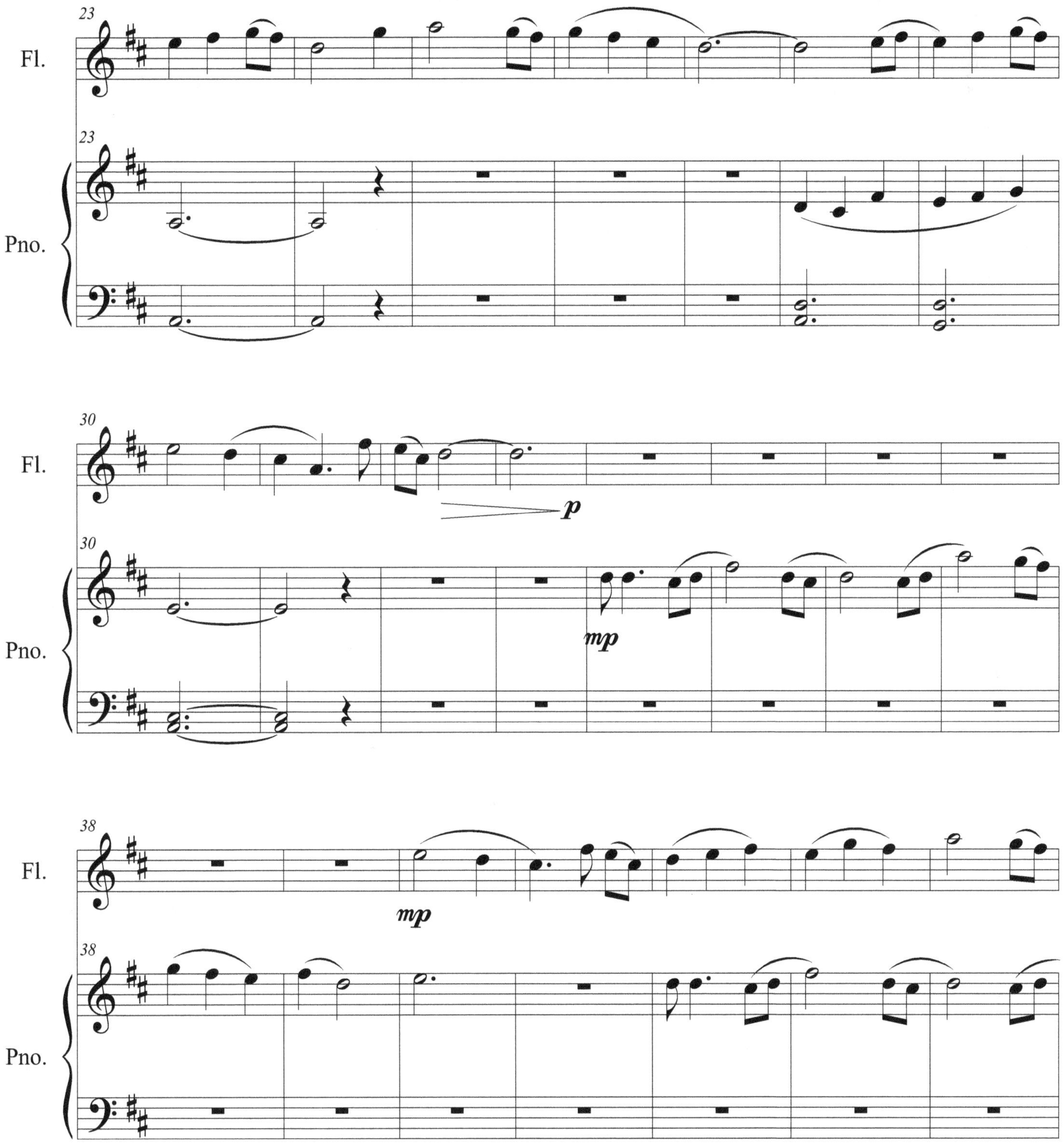
23
Fl.
23
Pno.
30
Fl.
p
30
Pno.
mp
38
Fl.
mp
38
Pno.

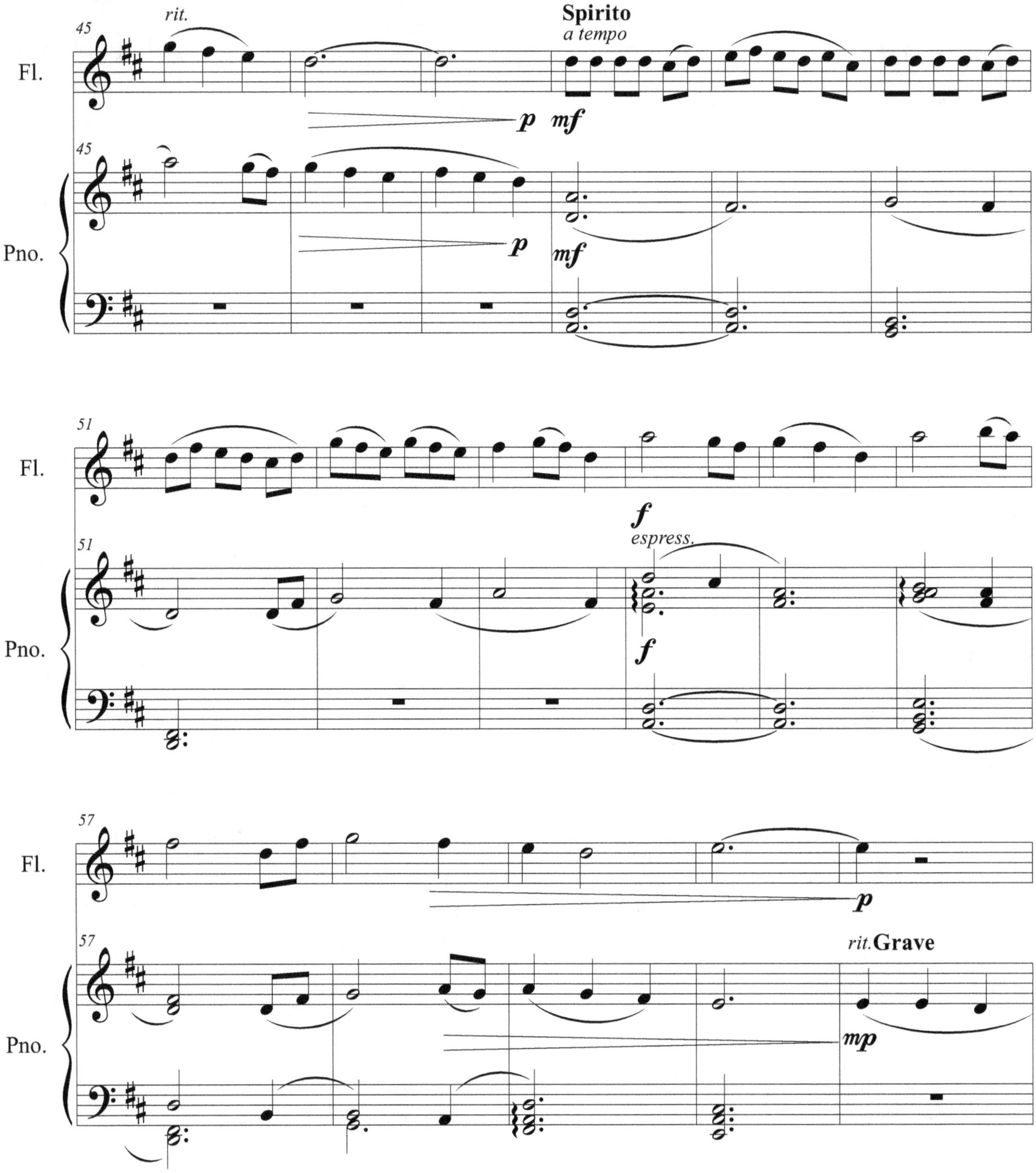
rit.
Spirito
a tempo
Fl.
Pno.
p mf
espress.
f
rit. Grave
mp

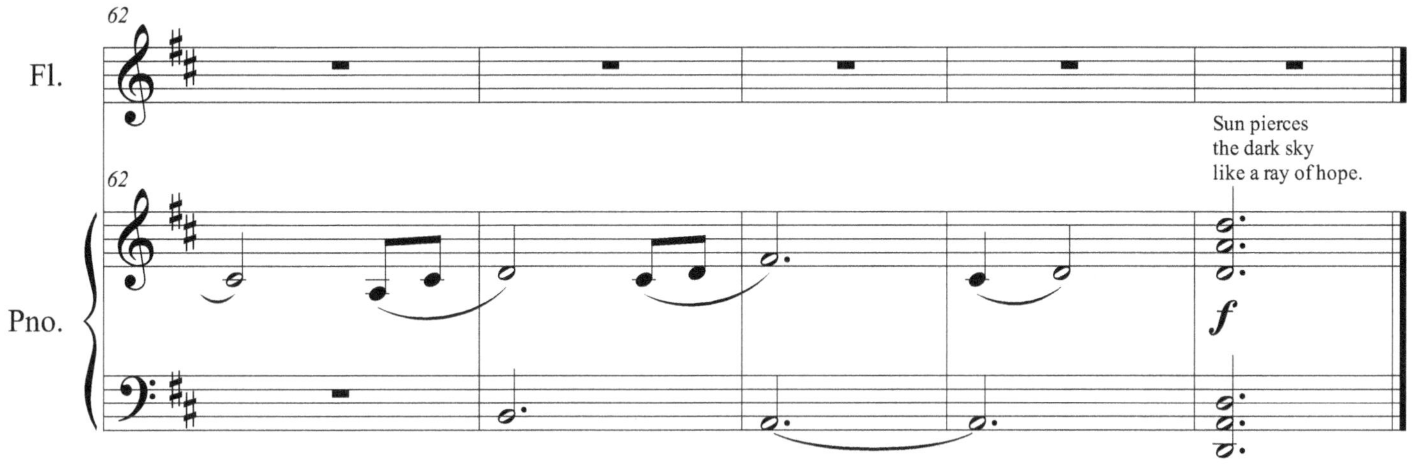
62
Fl.
62
Pno.
Sun pierces
the dark sky
like a ray of hope.
f

Flute

Flute

Hope

Xavier Hersom

Sun pierces
the dark sky
like a ray of hope.

©2020

Piano

Hope

Xavier Hersom

Adagio ♩ = 100

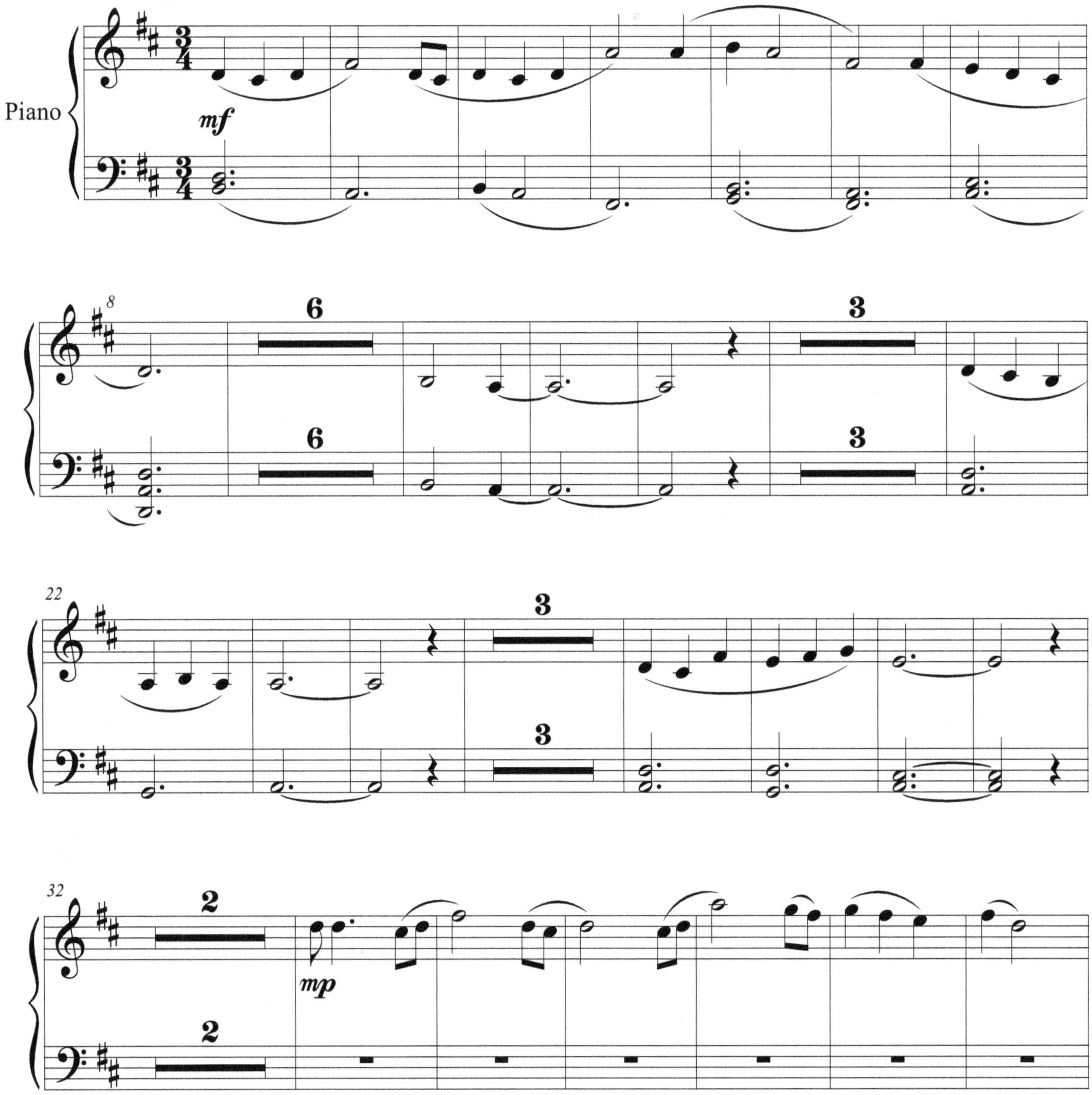

Hope

Sun pierces
the dark sky
like a ray of hope.

Listen to a performance here:

About the Composer

Xavier Hersom (b.1995) is an international-award-winning American composer. Though influenced by tonal music of the Romantic period, Hersom's compositions are inspired by current national issues. He believes art enables people to see the world from other perspectives and that music can spread awareness of social injustices. Learn more about him at:

www.XavierHersom.com

If you enjoy this music, please consider leaving a review.
Thank you!